WILD WEATHER

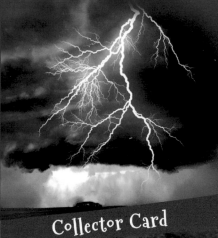

Collector Card

WILD WEATHER

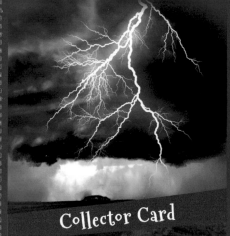

Collector Card

WILD WEATHER

Collector Card

WILD WEATHER

Collector Card

Tornado

A tornado, or twister, picks up or destroys everything in its path.

SCORE

DESTRUCTION: like a bomb blast	9
POSITIVE FORCE: none	0
AREA COVERED: path of about 2 km	2
FREQUENCY:	8

Bushfire

High winds and temperatures turn a tiny spark into a deadly blaze.

SCORE

DESTRUCTION: burns everything	9
POSITIVE FORCE: encourages plants	2
AREA COVERED: vast areas destroyed	8
FREQUENCY:	8

Ice Storm

Freezing rain creates black ice on roads and pulls down power lines.

SCORE

DESTRUCTION: trees, pylons	4
POSITIVE FORCE: beautiful scenery	6
AREA COVERED: large areas	6
FREQUENCY:	4

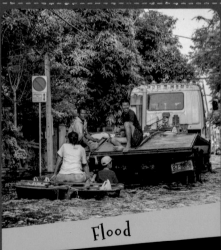

Flood

Houses and streets fill with mud and sewage during severe floods.

SCORE

DESTRUCTION: houses ruined	7
POSITIVE FORCE: none	0
AREA COVERED: large areas	6
FREQUENCY:	3

It's all about…

WILD
WEATHER

KINGFISHER

KINGFISHER

First published 2015 by Kingfisher
an imprint of Pan Macmillan
20 New Wharf Road, London N1 9RR
Associated companies throughout the world
www.panmacmillan.com

Series editor: Sarah Snashall
Series design: Little Red Ant
Adapted from an original text by Anita Ganeri

ISBN 978-0-7534-3890-9

9 8 7 6 5 4 3 2 1

1SP/1215/MPA/UG/128MA

A CIP catalogue record for this book is available from the British Library.

Printed in China

Picture credits
The Publisher would like to thank the following for permission to reproduce their material.
Top = t; Bottom = b; Centre = c; Left = l; Right = r
Cover Shutterstock/Minerva Studio, Shutterstock/Denis Rozhnovsky; Back cover
Shutterstock/Gary Paul Lewis; Pages 4 Shutterstock/BlueOrange Studio; 5t Shutterstock/
Sumet Boasin; 5b Shutterstock/photomatz; 6–7 Kingfisher Artbank; 7 Shutterstock/Francois
Etienne du Plessis; 8 Shutterstock/Steve Smith; 9 NASA; 9c Shutterstock/Stephen Meese;
10–11 Shutterstock/Bern Leitner Fotodesign; 11 Shutterstock/Nicram Sabod;
12–13 Kingfisher Artbank; 13 Shutterstock/andreiuc88; 14 Shutterstock/Daniel Loretto;
15 Shutterstock/Yuri4u80; 15t photolib.noaa.gov/Historic NWS Collection; 16–17
Shutterstock/EmiliaUngur; 17 Getty/Ed Darack; 18 Shutterstock/Jostein Hauge; 19 SPL/Pekka
Parvianen; 20–21 Shutterstock/Yoann Combronde; 21t Shutterstock/Denis Burdin; 22 SPL/
David Hay Jones; 23 Shutterstock/3Dsculptor; 23t SPL/NASA/JPL/Caltech; 24 Flickr/NASA/
Jeff Schmaltz; 25 Shutterstock/Ververidis Vasilis; 26 Shutterstock/Valery Shanin;
26–27 Shutterstock/szefei; 27t Shutterstock/Stephane Bidouze; 27c Shutterstock/Bernhard
Staehli; 27b Shutterstock/Ensuper; 28 Shutterstock/Janelle Lugge; 29 Shutterstock/
hessianmercenary; 29t SPL/Jim Reed Photography; 32 Shutterstock/Bernhard Staehl.
Cards: Front tl Getty/Cultura Science/Jason Persoff Stormdoctor; tr Shutterstock/Lindsay
Basson; bl Shutterstock/Ioan Florin Cnejevici; br Shutterstock/Karnt Thassanphak;
Back tl Shutterstock/Sytillin Pavel; tr NASA; bl Shutterstock/Dennis van de Water;
br Shutterstock/OlgaLis.

Front cover: Lightning strikes over dark storm clouds.

CONTENTS

For your free audio download go to
http://panmacmillan.com/WildWeather
or goo.gl/u4UZdj
Happy listening!

Too much weather

What is the weather like today? Sunny or snowy? Windy or rainy? Most types of weather can be fun, but too much of any one kind of weather can be a disaster.

The seaside is fun on a sunny day, but too much sun can cause drought or bushfires.

This farm vehicle is stuck in deep mud after bad weather.

For most of us, the weather affects the clothes we wear and whether we can play outside. But for farmers, fishermen, pilots, sailors and others, the weather can be dangerous and make it harder to do their jobs.

Fishermen often work at sea in very bad weather.

A warm blanket

The Earth is covered by a layer of air called the atmosphere. It stretches for hundreds of kilometres above the Earth.

The weather happens in the lowest part of the atmosphere nearest the Earth's surface.

The thin layer of atmosphere around the Earth can be seen from space.

FACT...

The atmosphere traps in warm air like a blanket. The Earth would be much colder without its atmosphere.

Weather balloons collect information about temperature, wind speed and air pressure.

satellite

space shuttle

aurora lights

shooting stars

weather balloon

aeroplane

weather layer

This picture shows what happens at different heights inside the Earth's atmosphere.

The wind

When the Sun heats air near the ground, the air floats upwards. Cooler air flows in to take its place. This makes wind.

Cool air from the sea makes breezes and waves at the seaside.

When we measure the wind, we measure how fast the air is moving and in which direction it blows.

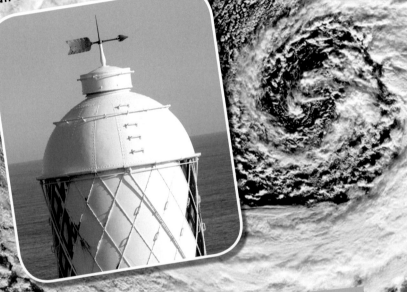

Anemometers measure the speed of the wind. Wind vanes measure the direction of the wind.

SPOTLIGHT: Cyclone Olivia

Record breaker:	highest-ever non-tornado wind
Date:	10 April, 1996
Wind strength:	408 km/h
Damage:	US$10 million; 10 injuries

Clouds

Wispy white clouds and lumpy black clouds look very different, but they are both made from millions and millions of tiny water droplets or ice crystals.

When cumulus clouds turn grey you can expect rain.

Clouds come in all sorts of shapes and sizes. Different types of cloud bring different kinds of weather.

Cirrus clouds are wispy clouds high in the sky. They show the weather might be changing.

Stratus clouds are flat layers of cloud that can bring snow if it is cold.

FACT...

Lenticular clouds look like flying saucers.

a lenticular cloud

11

Rain and snow

Water is always moving round between the land, the sea and the air.

rain falls from
the clouds

water soaks
into the ground

When the water droplets or ice crystals in a cloud grow large enough, they fall to the ground as rain. Snow comes from ice crystals that reach the ground before they melt.

When rain freezes as it falls, trees become covered with ice.

water vapour cools and makes clouds

water evaporates from seas, lakes and rivers

rainwater runs into rivers and back to the sea

13

Lightning strike

Lightning comes from giant storm clouds. Inside a storm cloud, the water droplets and bits of ice crash into each other, making electricity.

When there is too much electricity for the cloud to hold, the electricity jumps to the ground as lightning.

FACT...

Storm clouds can be 15 kilometres tall!

Lightning strikes the Eiffel Tower
in Paris, France in 1902.

SPOTLIGHT: Catatumbo, Venezuela

Record breaker:	most lightning strikes
Frequency:	160 nights per year
Rate per hour:	up to 280 strikes
Fact:	stopped January to April 2010

Terrible twisters

A tornado is a spinning funnel of air from a storm cloud. Tornadoes are also called twisters, particularly in the USA. As a tornado touches the ground, cars are thrown about like toys and houses are torn to pieces.

FACT...

Hundreds of tornadoes touch down every year in Tornado Alley, USA.

This boat was washed ashore by huge waves caused by a hurricane.

Sometimes, big groups of storm clouds near the Equator turn into spinning storms called hurricanes, cyclones or typhoons. Inside a hurricane are super-strong winds and heavy rain.

FACT...

In 2010, hundreds of small fish fell on a town in Australia! The fish were probably sucked up from a river by a tornado.

Colours in the sky

When the Sun shines through raindrops, they split the rays of light to make a rainbow.

aurora borealis

FACT...

An aurora is a natural light display seen in the far northern and far southern parts of the Earth. The *aurora borealis*, or Northern Lights, is seen in Iceland, Norway and other north European countries.

Sometimes, hot or cold layers of air form near the ground. They bend light in a strange way, making ships or buildings appear in the sky. It can make the sea look like the ground, or the ground look like water. This is called a mirage.

In this photo the real island is in the background and the mirage is upside down below it. The lighthouse has disappeared in the mirage

World weather records

In some places in the world extreme weather is quite normal.

Hottest place: Libya: up to 58 degrees Celsius
Coldest place: Antarctica: down to minus 89 degrees Celsius
Wettest place: Cherrapunji, India
Driest place: Atacama desert, Chile

Only specially adapted plants and animals can survive in the Atacama desert.

Antarctica is the coldest place on Earth.

SPOTLIGHT: Atacama desert

Record breaker:	driest place on Earth
Average rainfall:	1 mm a year; no rain in places
A dry history:	no rain for 400 years in parts
Terrain:	rocky desert and salt lakes

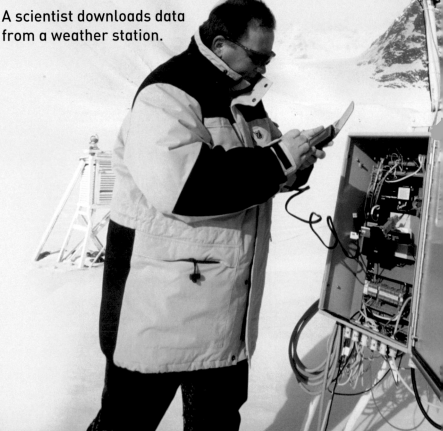

Recording the weather

Every day, scientists all over the world measure the temperature of the air, how much rain falls, the speed and direction of the wind, how long the sun shines for, and how much cloud covers the sky.

A scientist downloads data from a weather station.

The orange and pink parts of this map show the areas in the ocean with the highest winds.

Weather balloons carry measuring instruments into the atmosphere. Satellites take photographs of clouds from space. Radar can show where it is raining or windy.

a weather satellite high above the Earth

Danger alert

Weather forecasters use the information from weather stations to predict how the weather will change. They look out for dangerous weather so that they can warn people.

a satellite picture of Hurricane Katrina

SPOTLIGHT: Hurricane Katrina

Date:	23-25 August, 2005
Highest wind speed:	280 km/h
Category:	category 5 storm
Impact:	thousands of homes lost

Weather forecasters in Australia in the summer provide fire danger ratings. Bushfires can start when it is hot, dry and windy.

A helicopter drops water on a bushfire.

Weather patterns

There are four main types of climate around the world.

Polar: cold all year, with long, very cold winters

Temperate: four seasons, with a cool winter and a warm summer

Tropical: hot and wet all year round

Desert: hot and dry all year round

tropical climate

FACT...

Scientists believe that climates worldwide are changing because humans are burning too much coal and oil. This climate change is causing ice at the Poles to melt.

Places in the world look different because they have different types of climate.

temperate climate

polar climate

desert climate

Survival!

Animals and plants are specially adapted for the climate that they live in. Humans have to adapt too – they need to wear the right clothes to suit the local weather.

SPOTLIGHT: Thorny devil

Adaptation:	spikes on skin gather water
Lives:	central Australian deserts
Eats:	ants
Fact:	has a pretend head on its neck

This hole in the ground is a tornado shelter.

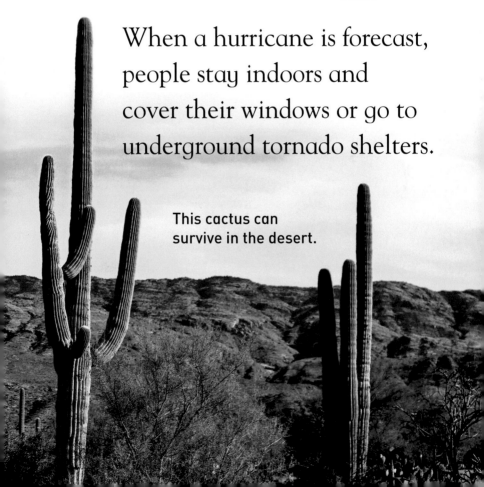

When a hurricane is forecast, people stay indoors and cover their windows or go to underground tornado shelters.

This cactus can survive in the desert.

GLOSSARY

adapted Suited to the place it lives.

atmosphere The layer of air around the Earth.

aurora Curtains of glowing lights that are seen in the skies in far northern and far southern places on Earth.

bushfire A fierce wild fire in Australia.

climate The normal weather in an area.

Equator An imaginary line around the middle of the Earth.

evaporate When liquid water turns into a gas called water vapour.

hurricane A big storm that brings strong winds and heavy rain.

ice crystal A very small piece of ice.

ice storm When rain falls through very cold air, becomes freezing rain and covers everything in a layer of ice.

Poles The places furthest north and furthest south on Earth.

radar A machine that shows up where objects are in the far distance.

satellites Spacecraft that move around the Earth in space.

temperature Tells you how hot or cold something is.

thunder A loud rumble made by a flash of lightning.

tornado A spinning funnel of air.

tornado shelter A hole in the ground where people go to be safe during a passing tornado.

water vapour Water when it has turned into a gas.

weather balloon A special balloon that carries weather equipment up into the atmosphere.

weather forecasters People who try to tell what the weather will be like in the future.

weather station A place where the weather is recorded.

INDEX

WILD WEATHER

Collector Card

WILD WEATHER

Collector Card

WILD WEATHER

Collector Card

WILD WEATHER

Collector Card

Lightning

Each lightning strike is a powerful second of electricity, sound and heat.

SCORE

DESTRUCTION:		2
POSITIVE FORCE: releases ozone		2
AREA COVERED:		1
FREQUENCY: 50 times a second		10

Hurricane

The biggest of storms causes damage with strong winds and heavy rain.

SCORE

DESTRUCTION: buildings and trees		10
POSITIVE FORCE: none		0
AREA COVERED: huge areas		9
FREQUENCY:		4

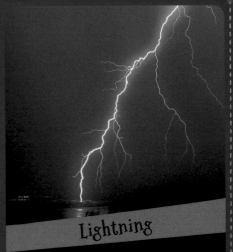

Drought

With no rain, crops die, wells dry up and people are hungry.

SCORE

DESTRUCTION: destroys livelihoods		4
POSITIVE FORCE: none		0
AREA COVERED: whole countries		10
FREQUENCY:		3

Snow

A fall of snow looks magical but it causes terrible chaos on the roads.

SCORE

DESTRUCTION: chaos in places		2
POSITIVE FORCE: winter sports		8
AREA COVERED: many countries		9
FREQUENCY:		10

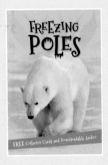

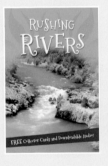